MY BIG SEEK-AND-FIND BOOK

priddy books

big ideas for little people

Find it

Circle the objects that match the description below each box.

green sock

yellow fruit

Hidden picture

Look at the farm scene. Can you find the objects pictured below?
Check the boxes when you find them.

Hidden picture

Look at the pirate ship. Can you find the objects pictured below?
Check the boxes when you find them.

Odd one out

One of these circles is different from the rest. Can you find it?

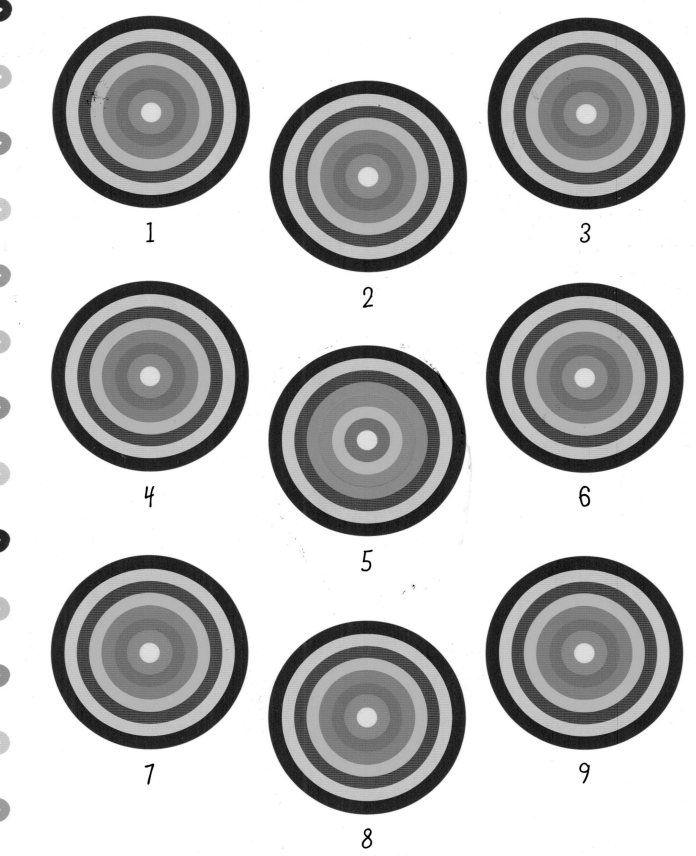

1

2

3

4

5

6

7

8

9

Spot the difference

There are seven differences between the two pictures of a cement mixer. Circle them when you find them.

A

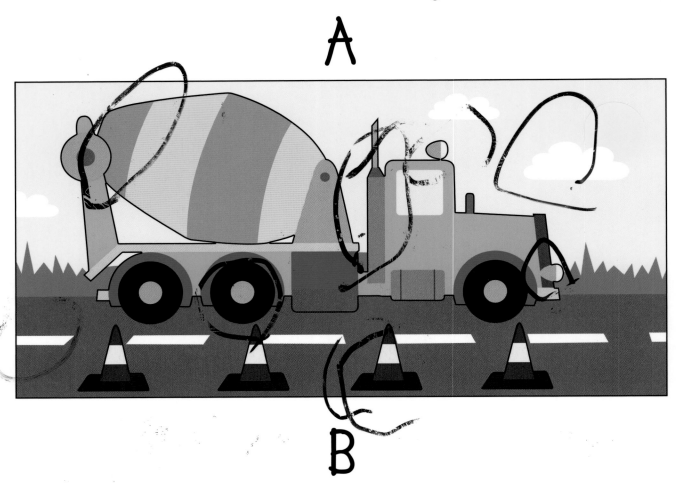

B

Seek and find

The toys below are all hidden in the picture.
Check the boxes when you find them.

Hidden picture

Look at this construction site. Can you find the objects pictured below? Check the boxes when you find them.

Find the detail

Draw a line from the pictures to where they are in the house.

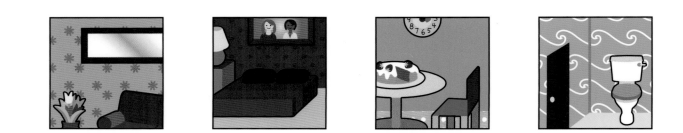

Farm maze

Follow the green lines to find the quickest way through the maze to get the tractor to the barn.

Hidden picture

Look at this coral reef scene. Can you find the objects pictured below? Check the boxes when you find them.

Odd one out

Find the teddy bear that doesn't have a matching pair.

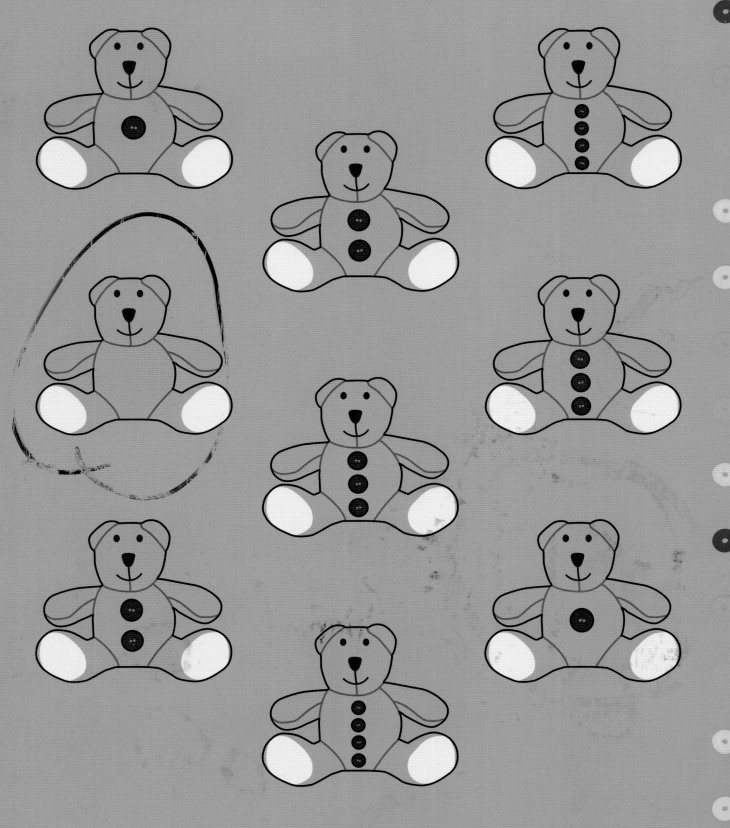

Spooky counting

Count and circle the objects below when you find them.

five shiny keys

four green toads

three blue potions

two hairy spiders

one wizard hat

13

Seek and find

The animals below are all in the picture.
Check the boxes when you find them.

Hidden picture

Look at the space scene. Can you find the objects pictured below?
Check the boxes when you find them.

Hidden picture

Look at this zoo scene. Can you find the objects pictured below?
Check the boxes when you find them.

Spot the difference

There are five differences between the two family pictures.
Circle them when you find them.

Hidden picture

Look at this store scene. Can you find the objects pictured below?
Check the boxes when you find them.

Hide-and-seek

Look closely at the stable scene,
and then answer the counting questions.

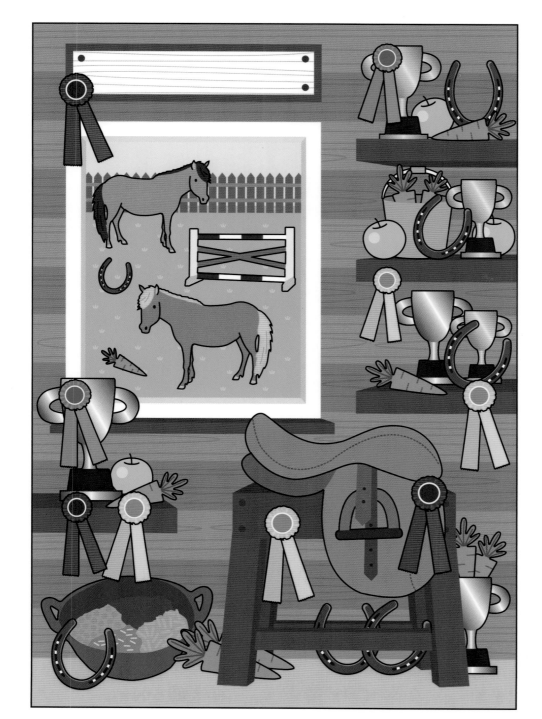

How many
horseshoes
can you count?

How many
carrots can
you count?

How many
ponies are
in the field?

How many
yellow rosettes
are there?

Toys galore

Count the toys, and then write your answers in the boxes.

teddy bears

toy cars

dolls

rubber ducks

toy trains

soccer balls

How many flowers?

Circle the T-shirt with five flowers.

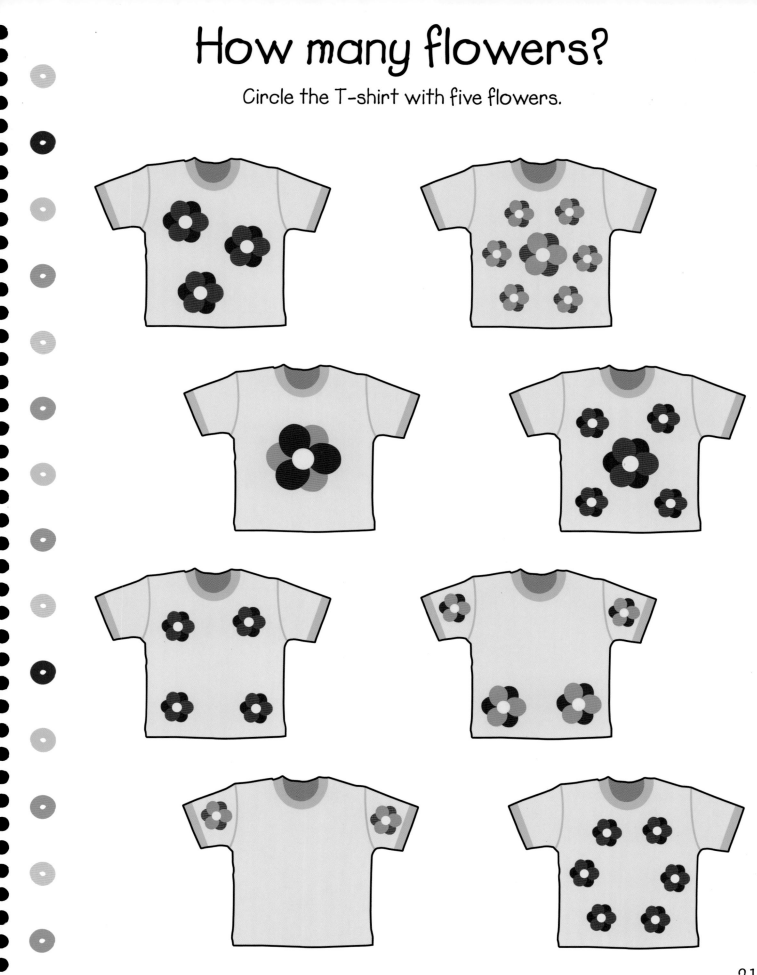

Who's missing?

Circle the bug that is in picture A but is missing from picture B.

A

B

Hidden picture

Look at this playground scene. Can you find the objects pictured below? Check the boxes when you find them.

What's wrong?

Circle four things that are wrong with this beach scene.

Yard search

Can you find the things below in this yard scene?
Check the boxes when you find them. Which one isn't there?

wheelbarrow	sun	butterfly

watering can	shed	bus

Find and count

Can you find and count the food items below?
Check the boxes as you find them.

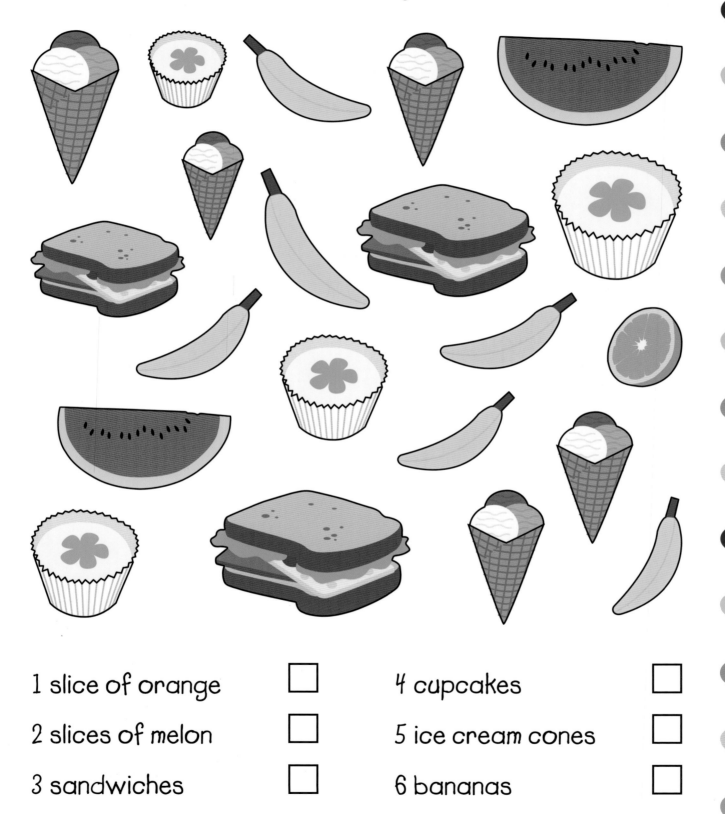

1 slice of orange ☐   4 cupcakes ☐

2 slices of melon ☐   5 ice cream cones ☐

3 sandwiches ☐   6 bananas ☐

Hidden picture

Look at this cowboy camp. Can you find the objects pictured below?
Check the boxes when you find them.

Hidden picture

Look at the barnyard scene. Can you find the objects pictured below?
Check the boxes when you find them.

Spot the difference

There are five differences between the two prehistoric pictures.
Circle them when you find them.

Matching numbers

Count each group of soccer things. Write over the numbers, and then draw a line to the groups they match.

4

3

2

5

Find and count

Can you find and count the items below?
Check the boxes as you find them.

1 sand castle	☐	5 palm trees	☐
2 boats	☐	6 crabs	☐
3 seagulls	☐	7 shells	☐
4 starfish	☐	8 coconuts	☐

Follow the trails

Which trail leads Misty the dog to her puppy?

a b c

Spot the difference

There are six differences between the two pictures of Triceratops.
Circle them when you find them.

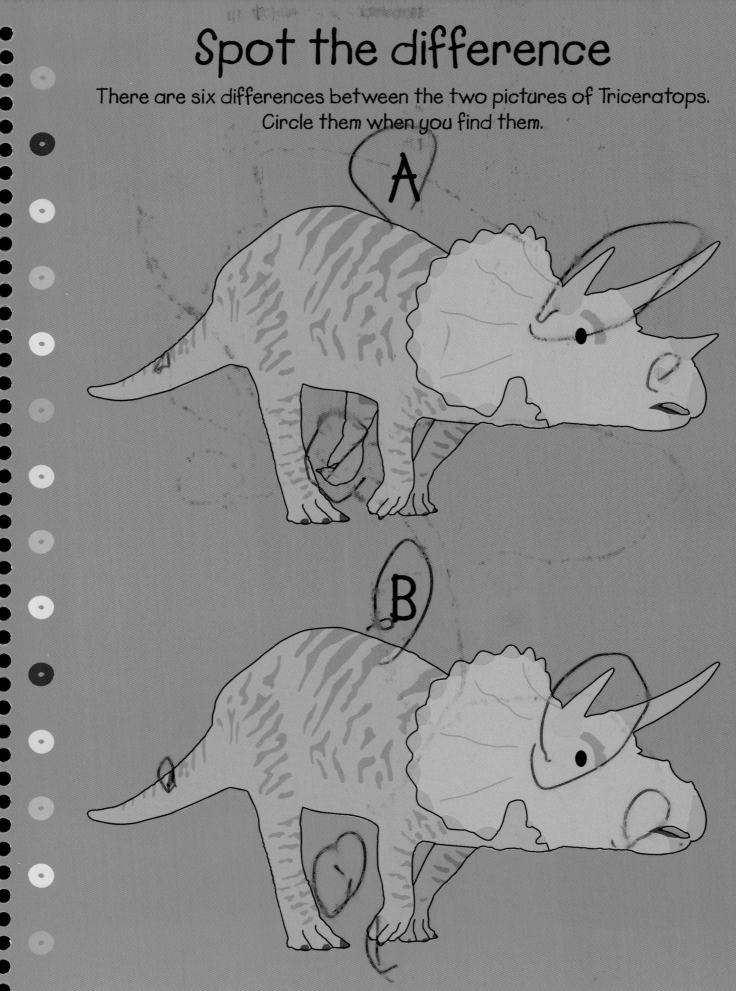

Hidden picture

Look at this ice cream stand. Can you find the objects pictured below? Check the boxes when you find them.

Hidden picture

Look at the station scene. Can you find the objects pictured below?
Check the boxes when you find them.

Matching numbers

Count each group of objects, write over the numbers, and match the two together!

4

3

5

6

In the air

Circle three things that are wrong with this sky scene.

Hidden picture

Look at this classroom. Can you find the objects pictured below?
Check the boxes when you find them.

Spot the difference

There are six differences between the two kitten pictures.
Circle them when you find them.

39

Matching pairs

Can you match the moms with their babies?
Draw a line between each animal pair.

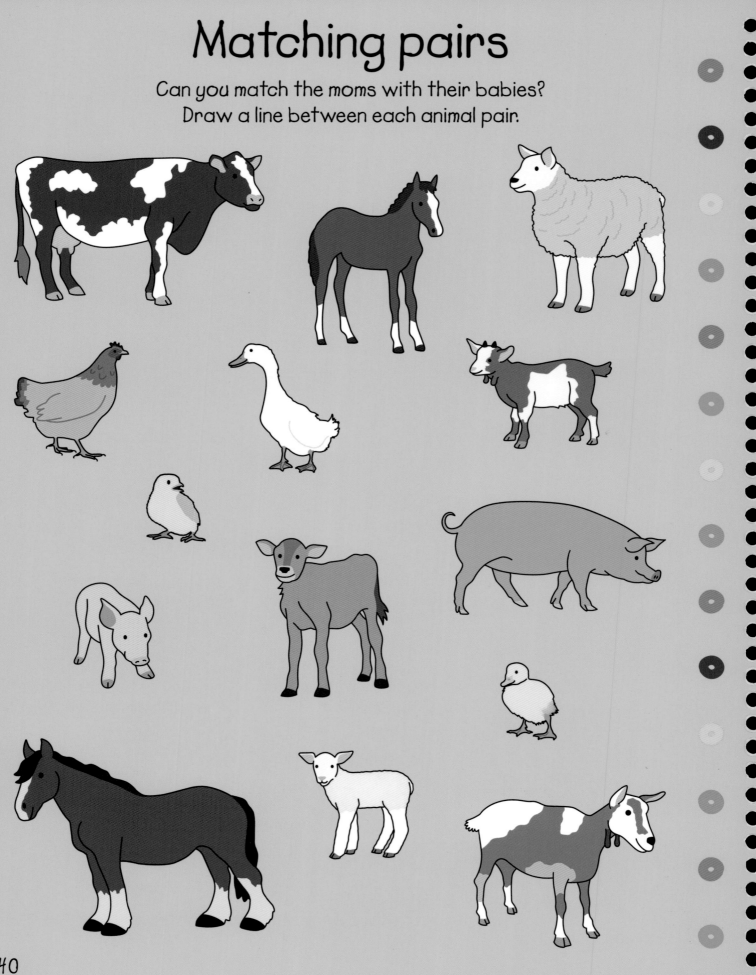

Follow the trails

Which trail leads Farmer Joe to his tractor?

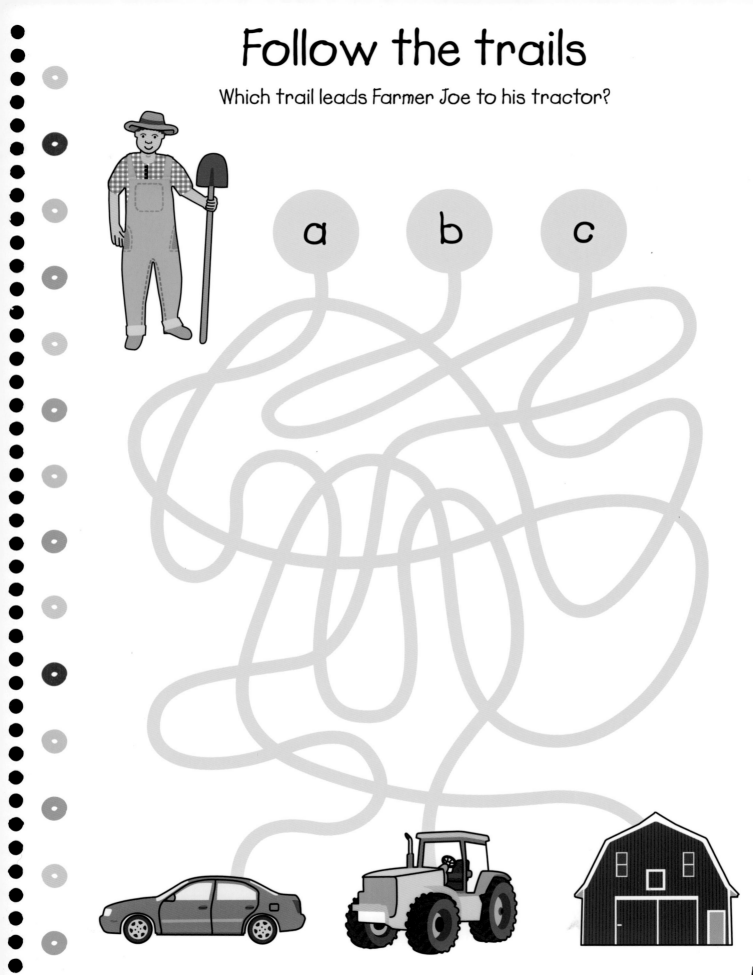

What's wrong?

Circle three things that don't belong in this yard scene.

Find and count

Can you find and count the items below?
Check the boxes as you find them.

1 cozy bed ☐   5 blue chairs ☐

2 mirrors ☐   6 clocks ☐

3 strawberries ☐   7 apples ☐

4 lamps ☐   8 pink socks ☐

Find it

Circle the objects that match the description below each box.

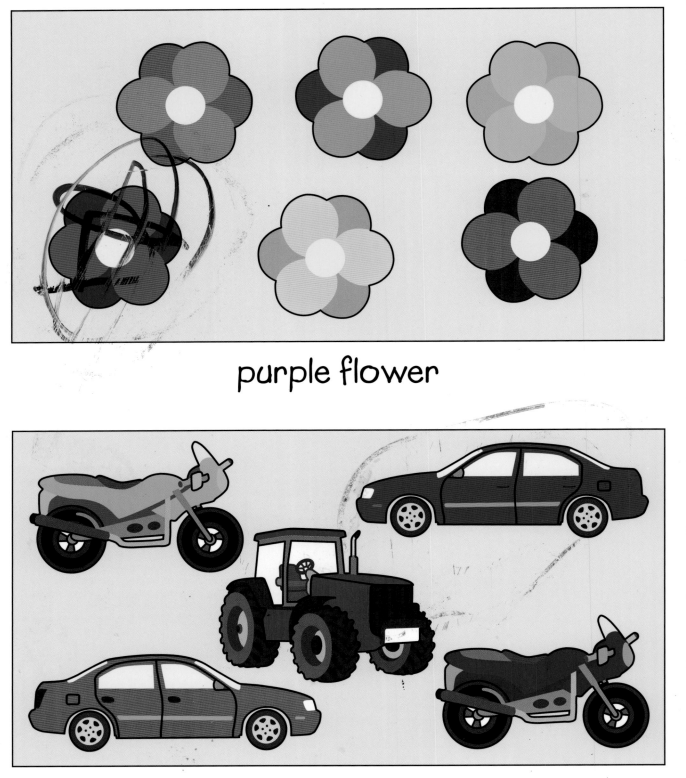

purple flower

blue car

Hidden picture

Look at the castle scene. Can you find the objects pictured below?
Check the boxes when you find them.

Hidden picture

Look at the picnic scene. Can you find the objects pictured below?
Check the boxes when you find them.

Hidden picture

Look at this dragon's lair. Can you find the objects pictured below?
Check the boxes when you find them.

Hidden picture

Look at this sky scene. Can you find the objects pictured below?
Check the boxes when you find them.

Seek and find

The sea creatures below are all in the picture.
Check the boxes when you find them.

Hidden picture

Look at the pet groomer's scene. Can you find the objects pictured below? Check the boxes when you find them.

How many?

Count the objects in each row, and then write the totals in the boxes.

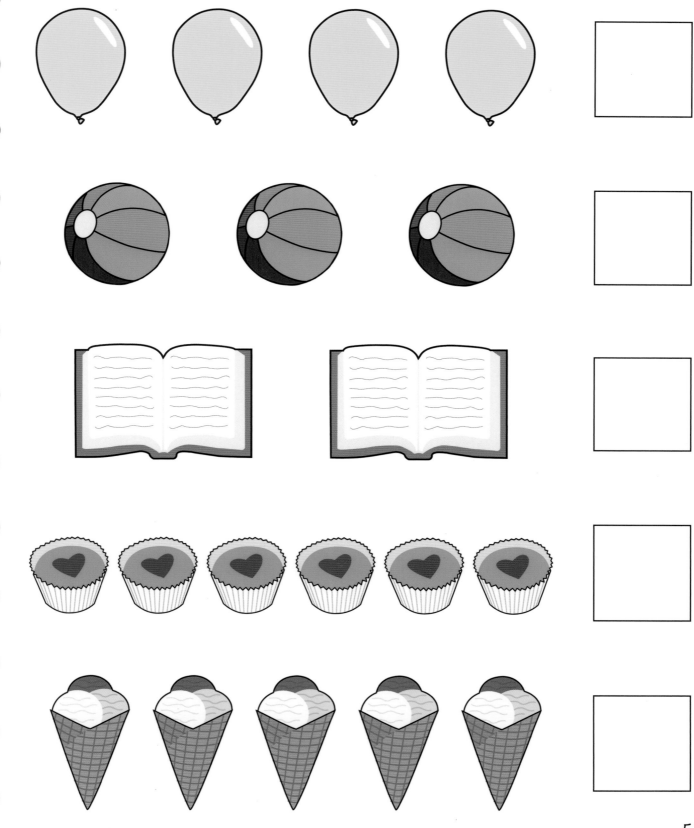

Hide-and-seek

Look closely at the pirate scene,
and then answer the counting questions below.

How many
parrots
can you count?

How many
eye patches
can you count?

How many
pirate hats can
you count?

How many
pirates are
holding
cutlasses?

Hidden picture

Look at this toy store. Can you find the objects pictured below?
Check the boxes when you find them.

Spot the detail

Draw a line from the pictures to where they are on the jewelry box.

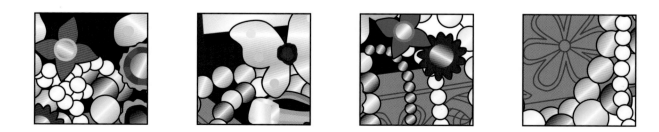

In space

Count the space things, and then write the totals in the boxes.

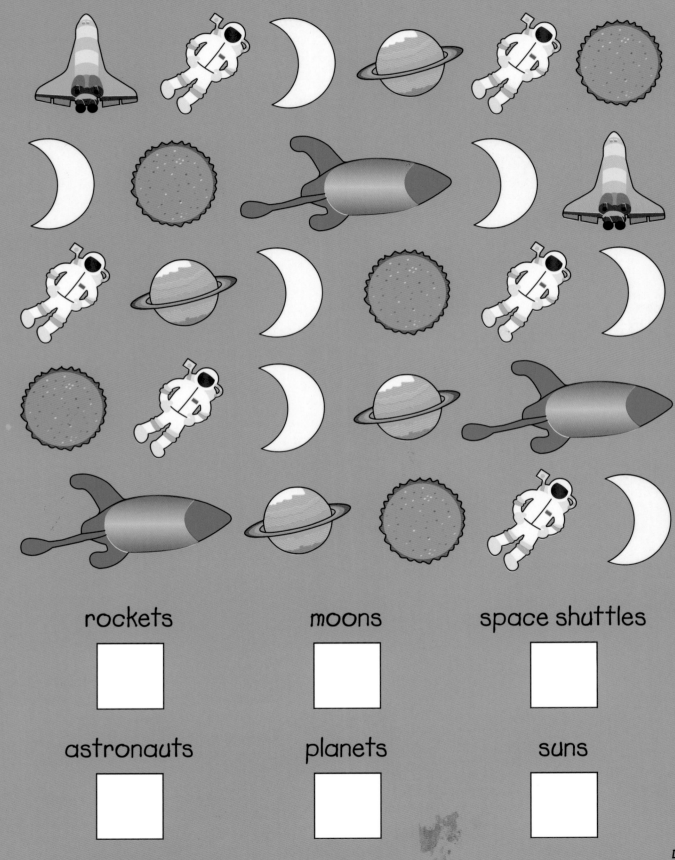

rockets

☐

moons

☐

space shuttles

☐

astronauts

☐

planets

☐

suns

☐

Answers

Page 2

Page 3

Page 4

Page 5
5 is the odd one out

Page 6

Page 7

Page 8

Page 9
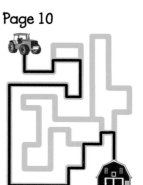

Page 10

Page 11

Page 12

Page 14

Page 15

Page 16

Page 17

Page 18

Page 19 – 7, 10, 2, 4

Page 20
3 teddy bears, 5 toy cars,
6 dolls, 2 rubber ducks,
4 toy trains, 5 soccer balls

Page 21

Page 22

Page 23

Page 24

Page 25

There is no bus.

Page 27